NO! DON'T TOUCH ME THERE!

BY GWARMEKIA LAFAYE
ILLUSTRATIONS BY PHYLLIS PARKS

My mommy wanted to talk to me today because in a couple of weeks, I will start school. I have never been anywhere without my mommy being there. She's probably going to tell me how to get along with others my age. Or, maybe she will tell me how to be respectful to my teacher by raising my hand to speak, and saying yes ma'am, and no ma'am.

When she started talking, it was about more important things; things that had to do with my body. My mommy said she wanted to teach me the same things her mommy taught her. She said, "Sarah, you will be starting school soon and there are a lot of evil monsters in our world."

I thought maybe she was talking about green, three-eyed monsters, but I was wrong. My mommy says that not all monsters are green, with three eyes. The monsters that she was making me aware of, were regular people, just like you and me.

Mommy said, "Some of them look really sweet and giving. They sometimes offer you nice things such as candy and gifts to make it seem that they are really nice."

"Some could be pastors..."

"...and some could also be policemen."

My mouth dropped in disbelief.
"How could someone be so sweet
and giving, and turn out to be
an evil monster?" I wondered to
myself.

"So, when will I know if someone is a good person or a monster?" I asked. Mommy said, "when someone is asking you questions about your body and asking you to keep it a secret just between the two of you; when they are telling you that you should never let your daddy or mommy know about what is going on between you and that person. That is how you will know.

There should be no secrets when it comes to your body parts being touched by someone without good reason."

Upon entering my room, my mom made it clear that sometimes the doctors may have to check parts of my body. She said that she would be with me during those special touches, and that I do not have to worry. Then she asked me, "what are the places of your body that should not be touched by anyone?"

Thinking long and hard, I answered, "my lips." She said "Yes! What other places, Sarah?" I answered, "my hips, the part above my stomach, my thighs, and the part below my belly button." "Great job Sarah!" Mommy shouted. "But you are still missing a part." Thinking to myself, I finally figured it out. "My bottom, they should not touch my bottom!" "That's right Sarah, that is right." My mommy smiled at me and said that she was proud of me.

"Sarah, what should you do if someone does try touching you in those places?" she asked me. "I should say No, don't touch me there, in a normal tone." "No," she said, "you should shout it out so that you can draw attention to yourself and that person." So let me hear it Sarah. Screaming out loud, I said, "No, Don't touch me there!" "That's my girl," she said.

Afterwards, she asked, "What should you do if something like this does happen?" I answered, "I should tell someone right away."

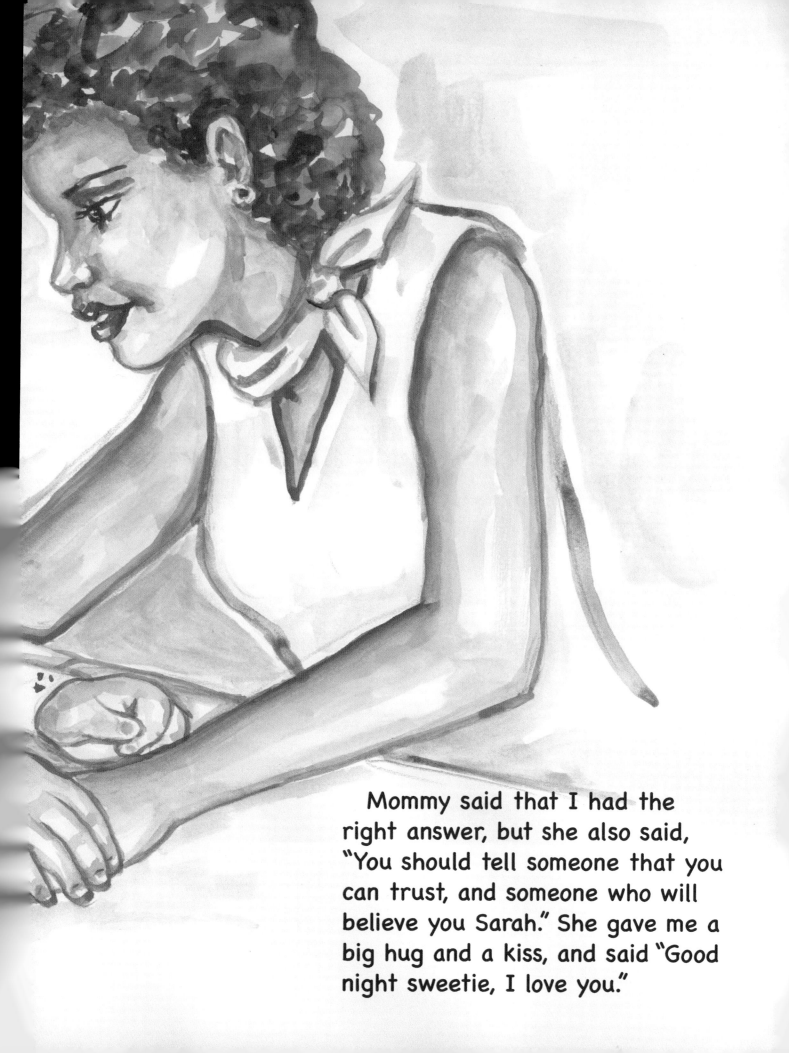

Mommy said that I had the right answer, but she also said, "You should tell someone that you can trust, and someone who will believe you Sarah." She gave me a big hug and a kiss, and said "Good night sweetie, I love you."

Now it was two weeks later, and my first day of school was finally here. The bus was waiting in front of the house for me.

I was a little nervous at first.
The thought of being alone
without my mom scared me.
But I remembered my mom said
that God would be with me, so
there is no need to fear. I walked
to the bus, met some new friends,
and had a great day.

Printed in Great Britain
by Amazon